A LITTLE
STYLE
BOOK

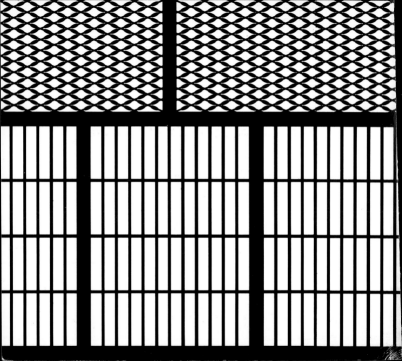

JAPANESE STYLE

SUZANNE SLESIN, STAFFORD CLIFF,
AND DANIEL ROZENSZTROCH

PHOTOGRAPHS BY
GILLES DE CHABANEIX

CLARKSON POTTER/PUBLISHERS   NEW YORK

Thank you again to all the people who allowed us to photograph their homes for Japanese Style; to our agent, Barbara Hogenson of the Lucy Kroll Agency; Beth Gardener, our editorial assistant; Ian Hammond, our art associate; Howard Klein, art director of Clarkson Potter, and Renato Stanisic; Joan Denman and Andrea C. Peabbles; and our editor, Roy Finamore, who made sure that this new Japanese Style, although smaller in size, was just as consistently strong as the original.

Published by Clarkson N. Potter, Inc., 201 East 50th Street, New York, New York 10022.
Member of the Crown Publishing Group.
Random House, Inc. New York, Toronto, London, Sydney, Auckland.
CLARKSON N. POTTER, POTTER, and colophon are trademarks of Clarkson N. Potter, Inc.
Originally published by Clarkson N. Potter, Inc. in 1987.

Manufactured in China

Design by Renato Stanisic

Library of Congress Catalog Number 94-20058

ISBN 0-517-88213-2

10   9   8   7   6   5   4   3   2   1

Revised Edition

CONTENTS

INTRODUCTION

Japan is a country that has long had appeal to foreigners, and modernists in the West have been greatly influenced by the traditional Japanese way of life. Simplicity, functionalism, and minimalism—three of the most important elements of Japanese design—have been honored since the 19th century, reinterpreted again and again by Western designers and architects.

When we undertook to create a book called Japanese Style, *we hoped to find homes that would help us understand the living styles emerging in Japan today. All of us involved—writer, art director, stylist, and photographer—had been warned about the reticence of most Japanese to invite anyone into their houses or apartments, least of all people who might want to photograph them. In Japan, privacy is sacrosanct, and "solitude is a status symbol," as Bernard Rudofsky wrote in* The Kimono Mind. *Entertaining nearly always takes place outside the home, and requests to visit someone's living space are usually responded to with polite refusals. So, our search for stylish interiors—whether traditional or contemporary—was time-consuming but intriguing. What we were looking for were homes that were somehow special—places where the occupants had made their mark, asserted their personalities.*

Nearly every interior we saw in Japan, with the exception of the rigorously traditional, suggested the tug-of-war between traditionalism and modernism, between East and West. Sometimes the conflict led to successful syntheses, particularly in the work of such architects as Tadeo Ando. His concrete buildings owe a debt to the International Style, first developed at the Bauhaus, but they also reflect traditional Japanese sensibilities and awareness of the natural world, in which the house is considered as one with the garden, and harmony and timelessness are seen as important elements in the perception of the physical world.

The traditional Japanese minka, *or folk house, with its rough exposed beams of kiaki wood often tied with rope, its thatch roof and tatami-covered floors, remains a powerful emblem of life around the family hearth. By contrast, the contemporary house in Japan—which makes its appearance especially in the big cities and is sometimes poetic, sometimes forbidding—reflects a more recent view of the house as a bulwark against the densely populated city.*

But most first-time visitors to Japan tend to look toward the past more than the future. In a country where the distinction between craft and art does not really apply, centuries-old techniques of making pottery, lacquerware, screens, kimonos, and calligraphy—Japanese crafts that are famous throughout the world—still survive as reminders of the continuity with the past. Many other traditions today are being rediscovered—whether it be constructing houses with wood joints rather than nails to express a reverence toward trees or creating complex textiles such as hand-woven silks laced with gold and silver threads, and elegantly patterned indigo-dyed cottons.

PRECEDING PAGES: *A glazed pot by Japan's master potter, Shoji Hamada, stands in the hallway of his house near Mashiko, outside Tokyo.*

THE LOOK
OF JAPAN

THE experience of being in Japan, whether it is on a bustling neighborhood street full of Sunday shoppers or in a tranquil garden created for meditation, is always intensely visual. By night, flashing advertising signs overwhelm the cityscape. By day, pastel candies and meticulously selected vegetables are packaged and displayed like rare jewels; a fish market becomes an aesthetic experience and as much a tourist destination as a walk in a palace garden; innumerable small restaurants and shops stocked sky-high with all manner of brushes, kitchenware, and chopsticks appear to spill out onto the bustling streets.

That may be because all these images are animated by the seemingly ceaseless energy of the people themselves—from kimono-clad women to blue-suited businessmen, from white-gloved taxi drivers to traditionally dressed farm workers who look as if they have just stepped out of a 19th-century wood-block print. In a city like Tokyo, observing people can be as educational as it is entertaining. Sunday golfers and bicyclists, festival celebrants, and neighborhood children all contribute to the varied fabric of the city.

Walls and fences, as well as such varied surfaces as a bed of red autumn leaves from a Japanese maple, raked gravel, glazed ceramic roof tiles, and tied bamboo, are some of the textures that add to the visual landscape.

While the crowds of people—including the trendily dressed teenagers who fill the popular back streets of Tokyo on Sunday morning shopping sprees and visitors who watch the punk rock groups at Yoyogi Park—are an important aspect of the visual panorama, sometimes it is the hushed silence and solitude of the Zen garden that encapsulates the look of Japan. The rock garden at the Ryoanji temple in Kyoto, created at the beginning of the 16th century, is considered the most beautiful stone garden in the country. The large rocks are like islands in a sea of gravel, which is laid out in ripplelike concentric circles. The simplicity and perfection of the landscape is the outstanding visual expression of the Zen philosophy.

PRECEDING PAGES: *Flashing lights and bright neon advertisements are one aspect of Tokyo at night.*

ABOVE: *Freeways zigzagging across the city are offset by the angular modern architecture of a Tokyo skyscraper.* **LEFT:** *The serenity of Mt. Fuji contrasts with Tokyo's intensely crowded cityscape.*

ABOVE: *Teeing off on one of Tokyo's multideck golf driving ranges is a popular pastime.*

Below: *The dense group of Tokyo high-rises looks like a child's construction of building blocks.* **Overleaf:** *Shutters and sliding panels articulate the façade of the* shishinden—*the residence of the head of the royal household at the Imperial Palace complex in Kyoto.*

21

LEFT AND OVERLEAF: *Typical Tokyo sights include people being entertained by punk rock groups at Yoyogi Park, a stern policeman, a blustery sky, and travelers on bicycles. These, as well as the maze of parked bikes, all contribute to the varied fabric of the city.*

Players try their hand at Pachinko in one of Tokyo's many game parlors.

Tickets for Tokyo's subway can be purchased from machines in the stations.

THESE PAGES: *In a city like Tokyo, where the taxi drivers always wear white gloves and sometimes white caps, observing people can be as educational as it is entertaining.* **OVERLEAF:** *Crowds of people, including sweatshirted teenagers, are a common sight in Tokyo, where Sunday morning shopping is a favorite activity.*

Baseball players, festival celebrants, a roofer repairing a tiled roof, a Sunday asphalt golfer, parents and children on a weekend outing, and schoolchildren and visitors to the Kyoto Zen Garden offer visitors varied glimpses of daily life in Japan.

ABOVE AND RIGHT: *A geisha in ceremonial makeup and traditional dress is an arresting sight.* **OVERLEAF:** *Bright red berries in a blue-and-white ceramic bowl compose a striking Japanese still life.*

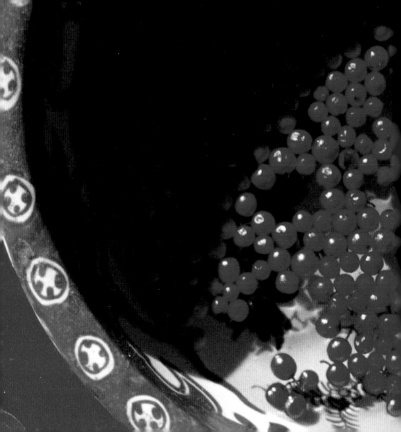

Overscale pieces of pottery—including some by Shoji Hamada, one of Japan's most famous craftsmen—are used dramatically in many interiors.

ABOVE: *Sticks of charcoal are inserted into the ashes of a floor-level brazier.* **LEFT:** *A spectacular antique porcelain bowl is set out on a table.* **OVERLEAF:** *In most Japanese gardens, the lack of space has inspired the creation of miniature as well as symbolic landscapes, in which stones are as important as plants.*

41

43

44

ABOVE: *A former rice warehouse in Kawaguchi has been restored.*
LEFT: *The roofs of the main house of an 1835 rice plantation are made of thatch or glazed ceramic tile.*
OVERLEAF: *Potted plants are crowded on a rooftop in Tokyo to create a garden in the sky.*

ABOVE: *Traditionally, porcelains are stored in beribboned wooden boxes.* **RIGHT:** *A collection of vintage Kabuki theater tickets has been framed and hung.* **OVERLEAF:** *Stacked boxes—often as important as the objects they protect—are kept in an antique chest.*

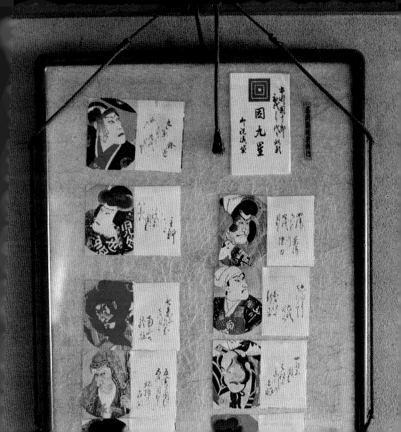

Tokyo's Tsukiji market, one of the important marketplaces of the world, includes more than 1,000 vendors.

Fish and seafood—fresh, dried, and frozen—are of the best quality. Shrimp and squid, as well as whole tuna, are displayed at dawn in stalls in the glass-topped warehouse buildings.

Sweets and shoes vying for space in a Tokyo alleyway, grains and beans, stacks of packaged chopsticks, and balls of twine are some of the wares available in mind-boggling variety from Tokyo shops.

The local broom maker working in his housewares shop conveys a timeless and peaceful quality.

Above: *Ukon Tachibana, an 83-year-old calligrapher, is one of the last to practice the ancient craft.* **Right:** *In Tokyo, a calligrapher reads the newspaper while he awaits customers in his shop. Examples of his craft hang like banners from the ceiling.*

An urban fisherman and a view of fishing boats on the ocean are calming scenes in a modern world.

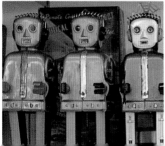

THESE PAGES: *Robots are part of Teruhisa Kitahara's extraordinary collection of mechanical men.* **OVERLEAF:** *Brightly patterned vending machines are ubiquitous on Japanese city streets.*

64

LEFT AND OVERLEAF: *The ancient craft of house building is represented in the peaked roofs of the reconstructed buildings at the Open Air Museum of Old Japanese Farmhouses, near Osaka. It is echoed in the details of new Japanese houses, including work by modern architect Tadeo Ando.* **FOLLOWING PAGES:** *Walls and fences, glazed ceramic roof tiles, tied bamboo—these are some of the visual textures of the Japanese landscape.*

LEFT AND OVERLEAF: *Dry candies usually served at tea ceremonies or celebrations are called* higashi *and* namagashi; *they are made of sugar, millet jelly, soy, and barley powder paste and are molded or baked into a variety of shapes. Some symbolize the seasons, while others are realistic and surprising interpretations of such seemingly out-of-context foods as clams.* **FOLLOWING PAGES:** *A bunch of scallions is securely tied to the back of a bicycle for delivery to a customer. Whether exotic or ordinary, vegetables available at markets are sold in formal and aesthetically pleasing bundles that become artful statements.*

JAPAN STYLE

THE tea ceremony and its ritual; the kimono, whether formal or everyday; the freestanding or folding screen, the architectural element that allows for and defines the flexibility of the Japanese interior; and the shoe-lined entrance that distinguishes the thresholds of the Japanese house—these are some of the intrinsically Japanese design elements that define the culture and whose interpretation is woven into the fabric of nearly every Japanese home.

Along with the enthusiasm for the current and technologically up-to-date, we discovered in Japan—and even in Tokyo, where nearly everything is less than 50 years old—a renewed interest in time-honored values. In pottery, one of the finest of Japanese crafts and one that is influential on an international scale, the functional is perfectly integrated with the decorative. The requirements of tea ceremony are one of the most important practical reasons for sustaining the craft. But nothing seems more evident in modern Japan than the influence of the Western way of life. Western styles in clothing, food, and especially in home design appear tantalizingly exotic to the Japanese and also represent a freer *attitude. Sitting on chairs around the dining room table, lounging on a leather sofa, cooking in an American-style efficiency kitchen, and collecting European antiques are only some of the common practices that reflect Japan's assimilation of Western culture.*

In the dichotomy between tradition and modernism, there is often a complex combination of two worlds. The guest room of a starkly modern house is furnished in the traditional manner, with a futon to be used by visiting relatives set down on the tatami-covered floor. Often the most modern of houses still retains a traditional tea-ceremony room. And whereas many foreign residents of Japan embrace the traditional Oriental ways, it is the well-traveled and sophisticated Japanese who frequently opt to live in a Westernized style.

PRECEDING PAGES: *During the day, a dining table and low chairs are set up in a tatami room; at night, they are put aside and replaced with a futon for sleeping.*

TEA CEREMONY

PRECEDING PAGES: *The contemporary tea-ceremony room was designed by architect Tadeo Ando using the woodcrafting techniques of ancient houses.*
LEFT AND OVERLEAF: *Noboru Kurisaki has a special tea-ceremony room in his Tokyo apartment where visitors come to learn the ancient rules of Cha-no-yu, or the tea ceremony, which include setting out the utensils, cleaning them, warming the tea bowls and small bamboo whisk, and preparing and serving the tea.*

LEFT: *Stone, sisal, and polished wood are the materials that define this ancient tea-ceremony room.* **PRECEDING PAGES:** *In a tiny Tokyo house, the roof of a tea-ceremony room is lined with goose down for insulation. A small cabinet holds utensils for the ceremony.*

K I M O N O

ABOVE: *When made of cotton, the kimono is worn informally at home; when made of richly embroidered silk, it is for more formal ceremonies, such as weddings and funerals.* **PRECEDING PAGES,**

BELOW, AND OVERLEAF: *Opulent kimonos are often hung on the wall and displayed as artworks. The marriage kimono with a bright-orange crane motif was traditionally worn over a white kimono.*

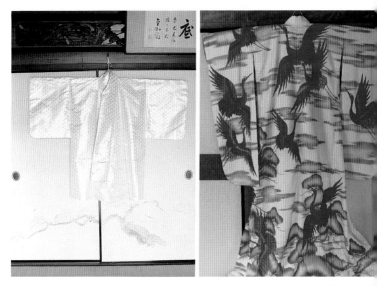

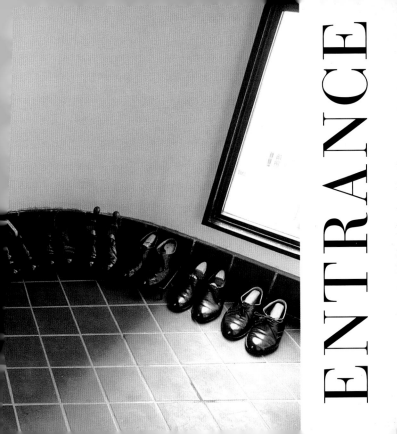

ENTRANCE

PRECEDING PAGES AND LEFT: *Shoes are traditionally left outside the house. Kimiaki Ashino's are neatly lined up on the black ceramic-tiled floor inside the front door of his Tokyo house, while two pairs of wood sandals rest in front of the black-and-white tiled floor of a contemporary Japanese courtyard garden.* **OVERLEAF:** *Shoes stand at the entrance to a traditional tatami-covered room in Tokyo and to a tiny Kyoto garden.*

ABOVE: *Slippers are ready to be slipped on inside the front door of a house in Tokyo.* **LEFT:** *The floor of an entrance foyer is covered with sisal matting woven in a decorative pattern. The window has bars made of bamboo.*

SCREEN

ABOVE: *A six-panel antique screen, one of a pair, depicts six months of the year.* **PRECEDING PAGES:** *A two-panel screen depicting women at work defines the stark entrance hall of a modern Kyoto house.*

BELOW: *A small screen is used to define a corner of a tea-ceremony room in Tokyo.* **OVERLEAF:** *Translucent rice paper, made into sliding panels or inset with leaves, is a traditional choice for screens.*

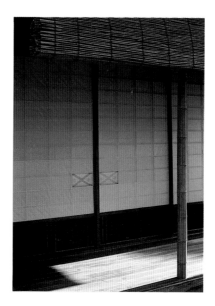

LEFT: *Sliding rice-paper panels in a tea-ceremony room in Tokyo are decorated with a pattern of criss-cross lines that are meant to symbolize rain.*
OVERLEAF: *An antique rice-paper panel depicting a landscape separates the living room from the foyer in a thatch-roofed house near Kyoto.*

In a traditional 250-year-old farmhouse in Kamakura, a wall of rice-paper panels lines the tea-ceremony room.

LOOKING
INSIDE

CONSERVING the mores of the past is an essential part of modern Japanese life. Taking off one's shoes before going indoors remains a universal practice. Ritual baths, futons for sleeping, low tables for eating, and tatami-covered floors for sitting also speak of the endurance of tradition. Although the television set is becoming a ubiquitous presence, many houses are devoid of the myriad decorative possessions that fill Western interiors. Usually the Japanese interior is restrained and orderly, and in the way that it recalls the calm and peacefulness of the past, it has become a modern classic in its own right.

We learned to become familiar with the tatami mat as a basic element of Japanese interiors. Measuring 90 by 180 centimeters, or about 3 by 6 feet, the tatami mat, based on the measure of a man, is used to indicate the size of a room. Advertisements in the windows of real estate agencies describe the common "two-tatami-mat rooms," as well as the rarer and almost palatially proportioned "twenty-tatami-mat rooms."

Set edge to edge in preordained configurations, the

straw mats are a timeless element that figures in both centuries-old and contemporary homes. They are also one reason why it is forbidden to wear shoes inside the house. "Upon these mats the people eat, sleep, and die; they represent the bed, chair, lounge, and sometimes table, combined," wrote Edward S. Morse in Japanese Homes and Their Surroundings, a book first published in 1886.

Making the most of a small area is a talent of Japanese city dwellers. The density of the population and the high prices of real estate have forced them to live in what Westerners would consider impossibly diminutive spaces. "A Japanese can make a whole life in a small space," noted Tadeo Ando, referring to the way even a tiny room can be arranged so as to provide all the necessary comforts. Important to this point of view is a willingness to live with only the essentials in multipurpose rooms, where futons are brought out of closets or chests for sleeping on at night.

PRECEDING PAGES: In a house in Tokyo, a large dining table is raised over a pit in the floor, which provides leg room for diners.

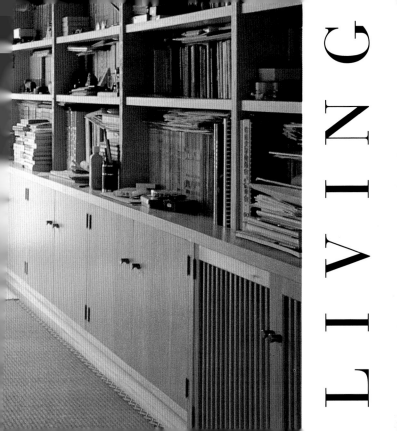

LIVING

ABOVE AND RIGHT: *Blue-and-white fabrics are used for the pillows and futon and to create a secluded tentlike environment in a Tokyo apartment.*
PRECEDING PAGES: *Ukon Tachibana, a calligrapher, works seated on the floor of his tatami-covered room.*
OVERLEAF: *Cane-backed chairs provide seating.*

ABOVE: *In the dining area of a house designed by Tadeo Ando, the end of the long wood dining table is cantilevered into the living room.* **PRECEDING PAGES:** *A large antique cabinet provides storage.*

BELOW: *In a Tokyo duplex by Shigeru Uchida, a large stainless-steel hood hangs over a cooking grill, which has been set into the table in the family kitchen.*

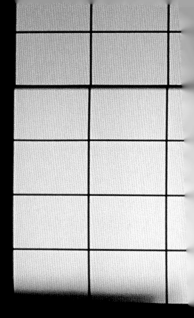

LEFT: *Sliding screens frame the combination dining and living room in a small house in Tokyo designed by Naoko Hirakura.* **PRECEDING PAGES:** *A traditional tatami-covered living space in Kyoto opens onto a garden.*

ABOVE LEFT: *A collection of 19th-century wicker baskets is grouped on a low table in an old farmhouse that belongs to an antiques dealer in Kamakura.* **ABOVE RIGHT:** *The porcelain figure is one of the objects in Noboru Kurisaki's Tokyo duplex.*

ABOVE LEFT: *A piece of antique fabric is draped over an Oriental chest in Michiko Kitamura's tiny Tokyo apartment.* **ABOVE RIGHT:** *The top of the small French antique desk in a house in Tokyo is covered with ivory heads and boxes.*

Books are piled high on the desk and fill the shelves of poet Matsuro Takahashi's combination study, bedroom, and living room in the Setagaya section of Tokyo.

ABOVE AND RIGHT: *A traditional-style room in Tokyo has tatami mats on the floor, a low lacquered table, and pillows for seating.* **OVERLEAF:** *Family photographs are hung above the sliding doors in a large wooden Kyoto house that dates from the first quarter of the 20th century.*

146

The shoji screen–lined living room in a Kyoto house is occasionally used for the tea ceremony.

LEFT: *A warrior's costume and two antique chests are at one end of the large sitting room of a spacious Kyoto house.*
OVERLEAF LEFT: *Antique Chinese runners have been laid on top of the lilac-colored carpeting in the gallery of a Tokyo house.*
OVERLEAF RIGHT: *Antique baskets used for flower arrangements are displayed in the small sitting room under the eaves of a rebuilt farmhouse in Kamakura.*

ABOVE: *Architect Takamitsu Azuma's island-shaped kitchen is all there was room for in his tiny Tokyo house.* **RIGHT:** *Kimiako Ashino's all-black Tokyo kitchen is equipped with an industrial stove and stainless-steel counters.* **PRECEDING PAGES:** *Large* tansu *chests function as room dividers.*

*Blue-and-white porcelain
is displayed in a cabinet and
on low tables in an antiques
dealer's farmhouse. Western-
style Oriental chairs are also
part of the furnishings in the
sitting room.*

BATHING

In Kyoto, a traditional wooden tub has been installed in a renovated bathroom, **PRECEDING PAGES,** and is also a fixture of an older house, **LEFT. OVERLEAF LEFT:** *A very narrow bathroom in Osaka has an open shower and illusionistic floor.* **OVERLEAF RIGHT:** *A Kyoto bathroom has a shallow pale-blue-and-white ceramic-tiled sink and a white antique ceramic tile surround edged with bamboo.* **FOLLOWING PAGES:** *A bronze sculpture of crabs and a bouquet of grasses create a whimsical underwater tableau in the bathtub of a Tokyo apartment. The traditional wooden-lidded tub fits in with the wood structure of the* minka, *or folk house, in which it has been installed.*

SLEEPING

In the traditional Japanese bedroom, tatami covers the floor, and futons and quilts are stored in cupboards during the day, to be brought out at night, as in a serene bedroom in Osaka, **PRECEDING PAGES,** and a shoji-screened room in Kawaguchi, **LEFT. FOLLOWING PAGES:** A telephone and clock are features of a more Westernized bedroom; a futon and pillows are layered over a mattress.

171

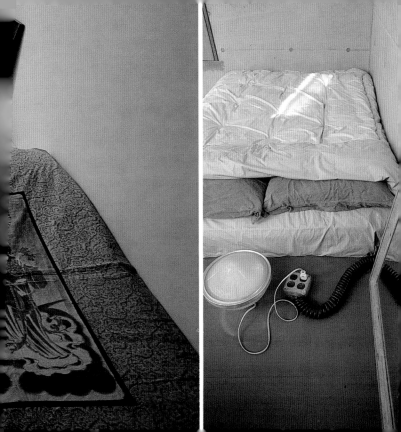

RIGHT: *The electric radiator, vacuum jug, and television set are modern conveniences in a studiolike bedroom in a Kyoto house.* **PRECEDING PAGES:** *Whether in a contemporary or a traditional setting, the bed—a mattress raised on a platform or a futon on the floor—is often made up with goose-down duvets and pillows.* **OVERLEAF:** *A comforter covers a futon. Futons and quilts are neatly stored in closets, ready for the beds to be made up.*

177

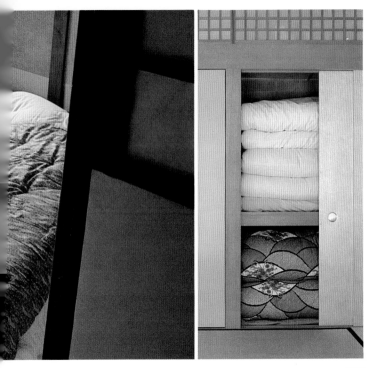

GARDENS

PRECEDING PAGES: *A Romanesque capital brought back from London is the central focus of architect Seüchi Sirai's Zen garden in Tokyo.* **RIGHT:** *The small inner courtyard and garden of a geisha house in Kyoto is paved with stones.*

BELOW: *A bamboo-covered well is one of the charming elements in the garden of a modest house in Kyoto.*

ABOVE: *Neatly clipped bushes line the stone steps in a Tokyo garden.* **OVERLEAF:** *Large ceramic pots are interspersed throughout the garden of a farmhouse in the village of Osumi.*

ABOVE AND LEFT: *At David Kidd's hillside house in Kyoto, a heavy stone lantern stands at the end of the garden, which was created in the 1920s.*
OVERLEAF: *Fall foliage frames a graceful arched bridge in a Kyoto palace garden.*

189

Carved stone wheels create a path in an overgrown and secluded Tokyo garden.

A thatch-and-bamboo fence delineates a garden where thick stone steps form a link with an open veranda.

ABOVE: *Sliding glass doors are often used to offer a gentle and flexible separation between house and garden.* **LEFT:** *Flat round stepping-stones create a graphic pattern in a Kyoto garden.*

In a residential quarter of Tokyo, low stools provide seating in
the back garden, and a large sculptural rock sits on a pedestal
near the house.

196

Bamboo—as screen or blind—is an aesthetic and functional choice for the Japanese garden. **OVERLEAF:** *A vase of flowers and a granite head are two of the refined touches in the garden of an old inn.*

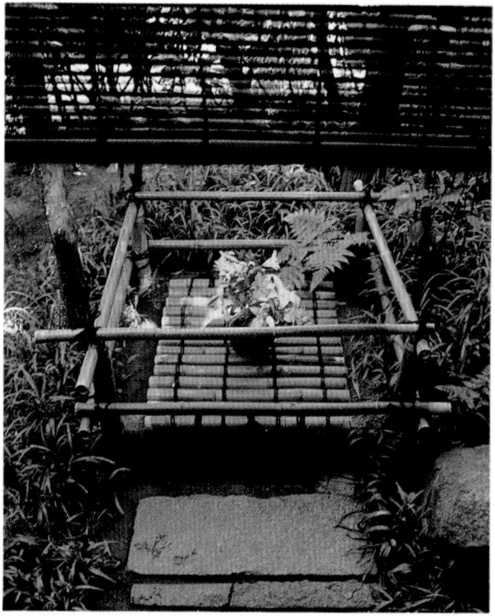

BELOW, RIGHT, AND OVERLEAF: *A Kyoto house and its garden, designed by Kazayuki Nimura, show how the two elements can be intricately linked. A paved walkway leads to the front door; the tea-ceremony room opens directly onto the exterior; and the focus of the garden is a pond filled with variegated carp.*

Other titles in the series